My Country
India

Jillian Powell

A⁺
Smart Apple Media

Published by Smart Apple Media,
an imprint of Black Rabbit Books
P.O. Box 3263, Mankato, Minnesota 56002
www.blackrabbitbooks.com

Published by arrangement with the Watts Publishing Group
LTD, London.

Library of Congress Cataloging-in-Publication Data
Powell, Jillian. India / by Jillian Powell.
p. cm.—(My country)

Summary: "Ajita, a young girl from India, introduces
readers to her country's landscape, weather, foods, and
festivals. Ajita also tells readers about her school, family
life, and things to see in India. Includes a page of facts
about India's population, geography, and culture"—Provided
by publisher.

Includes index.

ISBN 978-1-59920-906-7 (library binding)
1. India—Juvenile literature. I. Title.
DS407.P648 2015
954--dc23
                    2012042902

Series Editor: Paul Rockett
Series Designer: Paul Cherrill for Basement68
Picture Researcher: Diana Morris

Every attempt has been made to clear copyright. Should
there be any inadvertent omission please apply to the
publisher for rectification.

Picture credits: Neale Cousland/Shutterstock: 3, 20;
Dario Diment/Shutterstock: 11t; Nikhil Gangavane/
Dreamstime: 19c; Gavan Goulder/Alamy: 10; Mathes/
Dreamstime: 16; Holger Mette/istockphoto: front cover
l; Erick N/Shutterstock: 8, 24; neelsky/Shutterstock:
7, 21; Mikhail Nekrasov/Shutterstock: 11b; nrg123/
Shutterstock: front cover r; David Pearson/Alamy: 13;
Pawel Pietraszewski/Shutterstock: 5; Photos India Alamy:
14; pixcub/Shutterstock: front cover c, 4t, 12b, 17b, 19b,
22t.; Paul Prescott/Shutterstock: 15; Vikram Raghuvanshi/
istockphoto: 1, 6; Samrat35/Dreamstime: 17c, 18; Rikard
Stadler/Shutterstock: 12t; Przemyslaw Szablowski/
Shutterstock: 22c; Alfonso de Thomas/Shutterstock: 4b;
Aleksandar Todorovic/Shutterstock: 2, 9.

Printed in Stevens Point, Wisconsin at Worzalla
PO 1654
4-2014

9 8 7 6 5 4 3 2 1

Contents

All words in **bold** appear in the glossary on page 23.

India in the World

My name is Ajita, and I come from India.

I live in Mumbai, which is the largest city in India.

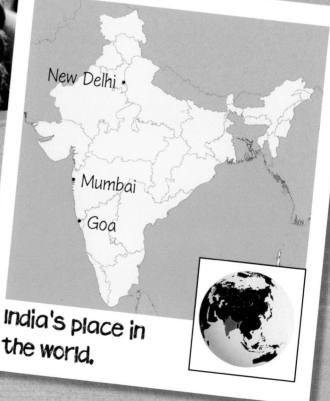

India's place in the world.

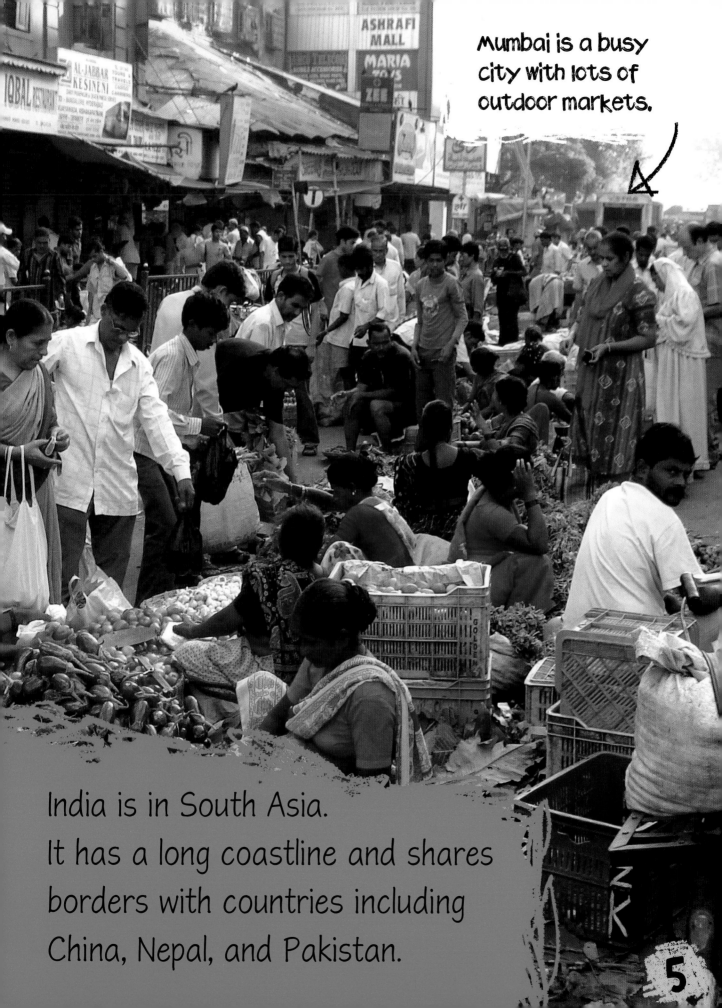

Mumbai is a busy city with lots of outdoor markets.

India is in South Asia.
It has a long coastline and shares borders with countries including China, Nepal, and Pakistan.

People Who Live in India

India has 400 million children, more than any other country.

More than a billion people live in India. Many live in big, crowded cities. Others live in small villages in the country.

Most people speak Hindi and English, but there are more than 400 local languages too.

Indians follow many different religions, including the Hindu, Muslim, Sikh, and Christian faiths.

This man is preparing gifts to offer to the Hindu gods.

India's Landscape

India has many different kinds of landscape from mountains and **deserts** to **plains** and **tropical** jungles.

Camels are used to carry people and goods across the deserts in northern India.

Almost half of India is used for farming animals and growing crops, such as rice, wheat, and tea.

The Himalayas, in the north, are the highest mountain range in the world.

This woman is picking tea leaves. Tea from India is sold all over the world.

The Weather in India

Heavy monsoon rain often causes floods. This man's rickshaw is caught in them.

India has three seasons—one is hot, one is wet, and one is cool.

The wet or **monsoon** season starts in the south in early June and moves north by July.

The northern highlands have a cooler climate than the south, which is mostly very **humid**.

In the north, the tops of the Himalayan mountains are always covered in snow.

Goa, in the south, has long, sandy beaches that make it popular with tourists.

At Home with My Family

Most apartments have balconies where people can hang their washing to dry.

I live with my mother, father, and sister in an apartment in Mumbai.

I like doing jigsaw puzzles with my sister.

I share a room with my sister. At home, we like playing games and drawing together.

Sometimes, we go shopping to one of the big malls and then go to the movies.

The film industry in India is the largest in the world. Three billion people go to the movies each year.

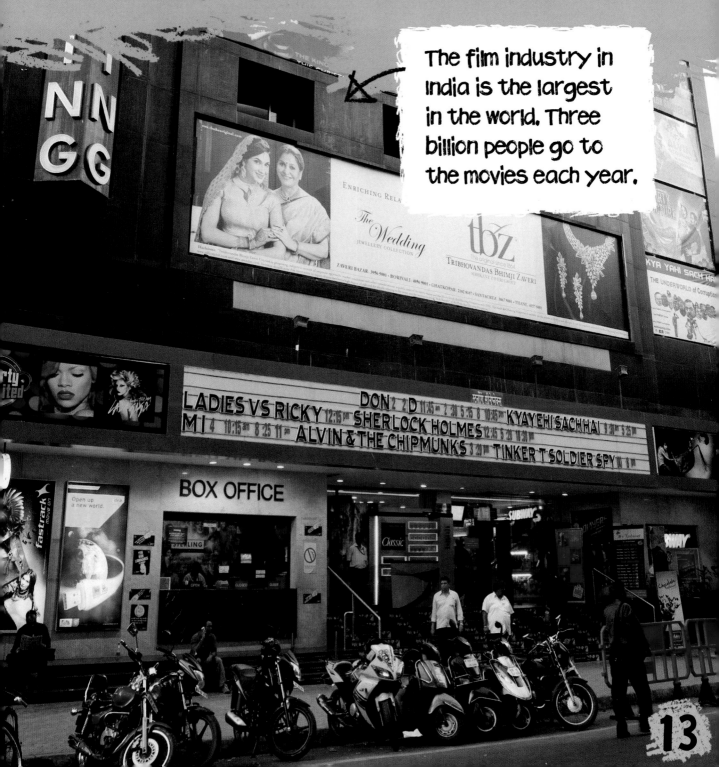

What We Eat

At breakfast, we have toast and fruit with tea or fruit juice. My mom packs me a hot lunch for school in small tins called **dabbas**.

These dabbas contain rice and curry.

In the evening, we all sit down for a meal together. We like eating **spicy** vegetable dishes with rice and also sweet milk and rice puddings.

Mom buys vegetables from the market. Like many Hindu families, we don't eat meat.

Going to School

We start primary school when we are five or six. My sister and I catch the bus to school each day.

Some of my friends take an autorickshaw to school.

We always start the day with prayers in assembly.

Then we have lessons in English and Hindi, math, science, and art.

Our teacher is showing us how to use a computer.

Art and English are my favorite lessons. What are yours?

Festivals and Celebrations

There are lots of colorful festivals in India all through the year. Holi is the spring festival of colors.

To celebrate Holi, people cover each other in powder paints.

Diwali is the autumn festival of lights. We decorate our homes with lights and candles and have firework displays.

People also get together to enjoy street carnivals and harvest celebrations.

For Diwali, people draw patterns in colored chalk or powder outside their homes.

I like Diwali because we have candy and fireworks!

Things to See

Many people who come to India visit the Taj Mahal, which was built in memory of an Indian emperor's favorite wife.

Over three million people visit the Taj Mahal each year!

Visits to the national parks to see tigers and elephants are very popular.

India has the largest number of tigers living in the wild.

Here are some facts about my country!

Fast Facts about India

Capital city = New Delhi

Population = 1.2 billion

Area = 463,330 square miles
(1.2 million km^2)

Main languages = Hindi, English,
and 16 other official languages

National holiday = Independence Day

Currency = Rupee

Main religions = Hinduism, Islam, Christianity,
Sikhism, Buddhism, Jainism

Longest river = the Ganges, 1,560 miles (2,525 km)

Highest mountain = Kanchenjunga in the Himalayas 28,169 feet
(8,586 m)

Glossary

dabbas small tins or lunch boxes that stack together

deserts areas of land that get little or no rain

humid damp

monsoon seasonal rains

plains flat areas of land mostly without trees

rickshaw a small two- or three-wheeled vehicle, hand-pulled or motorized

spicy food cooked with spices

tropical belonging to hot countries close to Earth's equator

Further Information

Websites

www.activityvillage.co.uk/india_for_kids.htm

www.bbc.co.uk/learningzone/clips/life-in-mumbai-pt-3-3/5912.html

http://india.gov.in/knowindia/kids.php

Books

Atkinson, Tim. *Discover India (Discover Countries).* PowerKids Press, 2012

Bajaj, Varsha. *T is for Taj Mahal: An India Alphabet.* Sleeping Bear Press, 2011.

Savery, Annabel. *India (Been There!).* Smart Apple Media, 2012.

Index